"*Crowned* is a declaration of spirit: the act of growing up fearless and curious— part country, part city—and spinning a yarn that reveals it all. Whether walking the streets of New Orleans, hopping a 4 train to the Bronx, or recalling the small-town Kentucky of her birth, Ellen Hagan's voice floats from one edifying adventure to the next, her keen poet's eye recording every essential nuance. Line after living line, *Crowned* sings with the earnest praise of home and heart."
— Mitchell L. H. Douglas, author of *Cooling Board: A Long-Playing Poem*

"Ellen Hagan is a twenty-first century elixir of poetry and truth. *Crowned* leads us into the mouths of lions and lets us slay injustice from the inside out. This woman-fighter-artist comes armed with the dark-eyed, heavy-hearted women of her lineage to give us poems rimmed with drawls dark as tobacco and filled with literary courage. We are weak-kneed readers finding balance in these lucid metaphors. Open your hearts wide for this brazen poet who casts her die with a distilled voice we should take the time to savor."
— Parneshia Jones, Conjwoman and Affrilachian Poet

"The poems of *Crowned* come from woman soaked Kentucky earth, the humid sweetness of New Orleans and the deep soul kisses of New York. Ellen Hagan's words trace the route of self with a tongue untied. These are a woman's poems, these are a bruja's stories, these are the incantations of a Roma woman. These poems are our maps home."
— Kelly Norman Ellis, author of *Tougaloo Blues*

"*Crowned* is a poetic collage from a life that has been ripped and torn in places and then put back together to create the portrait of a whole woman. Ellen's poetry tells complex tragedies and makes ordinary moments profound. And though these verses are Ellen's personal accounts, between the lines you see yourself, your family, and your neighbors. Ellen's retelling of her own pains and triumphs undoubtedly inspires you to reflect on your own. This collection of poems is a celebration of the human plight, a letter to the child in all of us, a summons to stand up and fight against injustice, and an invitation for all to rise to a royal state of being."
— Renée Watson, author of *A Place Where Hurricanes Happen*

"Ellen Hagan's poetry ripples with glorious sensuality and bold, vibrant rhythms that pulse from the page like a heart beating against skin. Her images are fierce with beauty and delicate with the violence of desire. She weaves personal stories of adolescent curiosity blended with adult ferocity. She possesses a unique voice that blurs the map of urban and rural, north and south. She writes the stories of America as the poetic geography of girls becoming women."
— Dana Edell, director and co-founder of VIBE Theatre for Women

D0611701

CROWNED

CROWNED

Ellen Hagan

SAWYER HOUSE
2010

The following poems (in one variation or another) have appeared in the following journals.

Connotations: "perspective. one pair. black flip-flops," "gianina bazaz. or mom"
Blood Lotus: "if names were prayers"
42opus: "crash of sleep"
Submerged: Tales from the Basin: "Young Thangs," "Times," "Bazaz Curse"
Woman, Period: "Reign"
PLUCK: Journal of Affrilachian Arts & Culture: "Dress Code"
Just Like a Girl: A Manifesta: "Our Women"
America! What's My Name?: "Plan B," "Conjwoman," "Break Me"
Check the Rhyme: Anthology of Female Poets & Emcees: "That Girl"
New Monologues for Women by Women Volumes I & II: "Intimate Lay," "II"
Muse Apprentice Guild: "IV," "V"
Get Underground: "Dear Lynddie"
Failbetter: "Old Bardstown," "At One"
La Petite Zine: "Old Lover"

The poems "Bazaz Curse," "crash of sleep," and "Rapunzel Redux" were broadcast on WNYC (93.9 FM, New York City) in 2008. Previous versions of these poems have appeared in theatrical versions in girlstory's *Scrapbook* and *Boxes & Boundaries* and in the solo show *That Girl*, which was performed at The Los Angeles Women's Theatre Festival in 2009.

SAWYER HOUSE
www.sawyerhouse.net

Copyright © 2010 by Ellen Hagan
All rights reserved
Printed in the United States of America

FIRST EDITION, January 2010

Publisher's Cataloging-in-Publication Data
Hagan, Ellen (1978–).
    Crowned / by Ellen Hagan. —1st ed.
    p. cm.
    ISBN-13: 978-0-9821560-2-5
    ISBN-10: 0-9821560-2-2
    I. Title.

Library of Congress Control Number: 2009939999

Cover painting © 2009 by Megan Clark-Garriga.
Author photograph © 2009 by David Flores.
Book design by Dan Bernitt.

ACKNOWLEDGMENTS

Crowned would not be possible without the following folks:

The Bardstown Crew: Kelly Wheatley, Lisa Forsee, Becca Christensen, Kate Carothers, Britt Kulsveen, Brandi Cusick, Leslie Crume. Without you women I would have been lost all through my growing years. So much love to you all. And Karen Harryman, who kept me loving my home and poetry.

Lindsey Homra, Melissa Johnson, Alecia Whitaker: The UK women. College and the poems from college—thank you all. Over and over.

girlstory founders and core members: Lisa Ascalon, Menaka Menon, Jasmin Morales, Chasity Seda, and Mauricia Mullings. These poems would not be as full of womanhood and grit and heart had I not found and worked with all of you. And to all the girlstory members still to come, I am with you.

Michele Kotler, Marina Wilson, Elana Bell, Rachelle Street, Renee Watson, Tanya Gallo, Jen Zwirn, Erica Kaufman, Zahida Pirani, Dana Edell. You women kept me in New York City. What a perfect buoy.

Kelly Norman Ellis and Naomi Zora Baskins for bringing this book to being. Mitchell L. H. Douglas, Parneshia Jones, and the Affrilachian Poets. What a strong, proud family I am so lucky to be a part of.

Heather Weston Bell, the Kentucky Governor's School for the Arts, and the Toyota Alumni Performance Fund. Your support has pushed me forward.

Kentucky Foundation for Women, Communty~Word Project, The DreamYard Project, Vibe Theatre Experience and Adelphi University. What beautiful places to work and be a part of.

Aracelis Girmay who was the woman of fire behind this book. Thank you for pushing it towards this new landscape.

Megan Clark-Garriga for seeing, truly seeing, this book. Your cover and you are such a gift.

Sawyer House and Dan Bernitt for taking such beautiful care of this *Crowned*.

Marsha, Domo, and Kevin Flores; and Amanda Brown: the extended family.

Gianina Bazaz Hagan, Patrick Hagan, and Michael and Jen Hagan: The Family. I am grateful always.

At last, I want to thank David Flores, who has continued on this journey with me. Forever I am thankful for your insight, love, laughter, talent, dance moves, and your ability to see. Such clarity you have brought to my life. Love, love!

CONTENTS

For all the young girls working their way towards woman.
Forever, I am with you.
And for my mom. Love.

QUESTIONS

Color—Pale now.
February skin torn through. Wanted always
to be darker, show the Arab, show the Italian.
But in the summer months, I darken, I do.

Ancestry—Back a while back, to Bluegrass birthplaces,
stone fences. Ireland. Never been. Assyria. Gone now.
Italy. My grandmother and Venice when I was 21.

Gender—Female. I shave my legs, my underarms,
below, but only when I feel like it. Took charge of that
finally anyhow. Girl still all the time faking woman.

Place of Birth—Elizabethtown. 30 miles from my home.
A dry town. No liquor, no way. Maybe that's why
I grew up so drunk all the time. But Kentucky still.

Sexuality—Lots of it. First knew when I was five.
Knew the reaches of my body even then. Yes,
I will take some. Comfortable wanting it.

Body Type—Skinny when I was little,
bony when I was young. Now my body curves out.
I got no breasts, but often when I look at myself
I am satisfied.

Race—Irish / one half. Assyrian / one quarter.

Italian / One quarter.
How whole am I with all these separate parts?
How many can I really claim?
How many do I really know?

Class—Upper middle, or maybe just upper.
My folks didn't have a lot early on, but now
my dad has car washes and hotels, a man of
bourbon and money.

Face—Large Middle-Eastern nose. My mother used to say,
"That is your Pop's nose." Oh. Under my eyes so black,
so dark. Try make-up and cover up. Try to understate
who it is I am.

Country—Well, here, America. There is not
one other place I know as much. Know its gas stations
and highway truck stops, know its cola and its plush interiors,
know warm water and no sting of nothing, America.

Religion—Father, Son, Holy Spirit. Catholic.
Mass every Sunday, but most of the time
my brother and I skipped to smoke weed, eat
Doritos and watch the afternoon spiral out from us.
Around us.

Family—Large on both sides. Mother and father
and brother, and Pop and Grandma and Mamaw and Papaw.
Tons of food and land. Warm sheets and soft grass. Easy flow
of the everyday. Everyday, I miss them.

BABY

At one I made my mom exquisite. I'm sure her heart swelled to the size of her vagina when I slid out from beneath her legs 12 months prior. It was November 1978, Kentucky. She told me I was shaped like a loaf of bread when under my blanket and that when she held me it felt like there were thousands of little marbles rolling round from the insides of my chunky thighs to the deep center of my rounded out earlobes. I was her first daughter, sliced directly from her gut, smelling of tap water and baby oil. I had eyes the color of the dirt my mother used to plant her tomatoes in and a swollen belly the size of my father's outstretched hollowed out hand. We lived together, the four of us; my mother, father and brother, in a split-level near the Nelson county line where I am positive I grew accustomed to the weather at an early age, six weeks perhaps. Heat in the bluegrass is humid, moist, dripping like the freshness of an outside shower. We had a swing-set, a sandbox, a backyard and neighbors. There were hand-me-down Batman pajamas waiting for my 2nd birthday and a courageous pummel off the city pool diving board preparing for my 4th. A brand new Huffy with a horn and a hot pink banana seat sat in the garage for my 7th and there was a boy who was standing in the shadows eager to break my heart in the 3rd grade. In the wings of the house there were meals we'd all eventually consume together, holidays where we'd devour red wine with our mashed potatoes and gravy and Easter Sundays spent chasing pastel dyed hard-boiled eggs all over the front yard. Behind doors there were X-men motorcycles and the only real Barbie mansion. There would be nights of keeping my brother awake for hours with tales of crocodile eating heathens and the fairy maidens that saved them and afternoons of raiding the cabinets for canned goods to play house with, my brother and I dressed as Lucy and Ricky. And much later there would be nights of raiding those same cabinets, just as my girlfriend's and my high was hitting a peak. There would be field party acid trips and moments of driving so drunk I'd almost slip into the bay window of our living room. There would be nights of hallucinations, bad sex in cars near 245, there'd be hitchhiking, throwing up, swimming naked, calling home from the police station in the middle of the night. There would be months and months of making my mother the ugliest she has ever been. But at one, I am sure I made her exquisite.

CHANT

My mother
Gianina Bazaz
a high held head, big nose
and all. Her 1970s hot pants,
pixie hair-do, the way she can
dance. Dancing, my hips, oh
my hips, thank-you. You have
been held onto, have fit into
tight jeans, have held up skirts
stopped fights, started them.
Oh, my green bikini, five years
old, my stomach proud and out.
Posing in the front garden
plants, hands on those hips
green bikini, frizzed out hair
the rolling hills of home. Kentucky
traces me, my body is hers.
My background, my state of
affairs. Hot browns and trails
the good things. Oh, ocean, the
sand I'd pour on top of my head
a blessing, a washing in the
waves, the topple over. The
starfish, the river trout, and
catfish, the bones in my teeth.
My white teeth, my lips, my
tongue to taste, my nose to

smell. Barbecue and
hot and spicy chicken wings,
guacamole with sweet onions.
My man's hands, goddesses
they are. Hula hoops. Hot
pink, jump ropes, long car
rides, 800 miles between us.
Single beds, east 7th street
mother feeding her child.
Eight years olds putting their
heads on my shoulder, long
walks to Red Hook, the
BQE in its industrial glory, fog
boats I've been on only
a hand-full of times, the east
village, the east river
the middle east not yet
traveled to, Venice, and
pizza on the canal with
my best friend since I was two.
Women friends, so many
I can never count, no bras
loose jeans, orgasms, oh
orgasms, you are goddesses
double time. Pot-pies,
fried cornbread, children
screaming in joy.
New Orleans crawfish, suck
da heads, the Marigny, Tremé
Old Bardstown Road, river trout

river trout, and catfish, Valencia
Street in San Francisco, The Mission
where we ate tortillas and burritos
leather pants I've never owned
grease lightning, school dances
going parking, kissing for the
first time. Learning to love coffee
sleeping late, egg and cheese sandwiches.
My birthday, new years aching
in this world.

PERSPECTIVE. ONE PAIR. BLACK FLIP-FLOPS

you were a girl still.
tank tops for every occasion.
salami sandwiches for lunch and
menthol cigarettes with tight
white-shirted boys at dinner.
wasn't the sitting in place, and
walking nowhere, magnificent?
not the right word? no. it
was brutal. no? maybe i'll need
a thesaurus. but you were
tanned legs and the kind of girl
who'd go anywhere. with any-
one. once. once you almost lost one
of me at sea. your clothes shed. your
curfew done, and you in the ocean, with
a boy who was not yours. but who
would have been able to keep you
anyway? and how i hate saying this,
but who would have wanted to
then? all nights of hitchhiking, halu-
cinations, tongues in mouths,
fists, fights and fast girlfriends.
none. none faster than you.

THE BAZAZ CURSE

As a baby I had a cloud of hair
that followed me.
It wasn't so much curly
as it was soft and puffy.
I looked so much like my older brother
everyone thought we were twins.
Once at the pool someone asked
my mother
why anyone would dress a little boy
in a girl's bathing suit. I didn't know enough
to be mortified and even when
my mother
tried to convince me to let my
hair grow long I wouldn't budge. I liked
the way I looked. But in the third grade
when everyone else was letting their hair
grow long and luscious,
I had my mom give me a haircut,
short in the front, long in the back,
which seemed the easiest cut to manage. And I
was in serious love with that hair-cut,
until Jessica Daniels told me I looked like
a freak with a mullet.
Oh. I hadn't noticed.
And that was just it.

"All Bazaz women have bad hair,"

my mother
said, pushing shoving
her own hair flat onto her head.

That night I dreamt of silky, smooth locks
I could fold out and lure boys with.
Smooth strands to wrap
slow around my fingers.
Twirling.
Seducing.
But my hair was a puff of awkward,
jumping two-step
out from my scalp.
Frizzed out it'd blow up two times
its size in the summertime. Still, it was mine.
Middle-Eastern, Irish, and Italian roots
stuck thick out.

ON THE BIRTH OF LIPSTICK

I

my lips straining for the blush
chapped cherry blossom, rouged up
rose-bud. peony. violet. the violent
pucker. honeysuckle. hyacinth. savage.
sliced watermelon. juices training around
pout. fleshy mango. pulp of blood orange.
mouth, a syrupy ache. all fruit. flowered.
bloomed out.

II

i pocketed my neighbor emily's play
gloss and wore it to bed with me
nights when it was clear my tongue
would lay dormant for many more
years. puckered still. my mouth a garden.
an orchard. i'd wait.

REIGN

It was a Saturday afternoon, sun aching in the sky,
my one piece hugged tight around me, fast
a fish below the surface, my strokes quick.
10 years old, whipping circles in our pool,
new, backstroke and butterfly my
specialties, my blue ribbons at town swim meets.
Still played house, and Barbie, rode my bike zig-zag around
the drive, made the hot pink hula-hoop jitter around my
un-grown, un-woman hips, still.
Still, I was shocked by the blood. No reading or
stories could prep me, stuck in my parents' bathroom,
the color of rust, soaking through my first fire-red Speedo.
A cut or wound, I searched my thighs for the spot,
threw off my suit and cried, called my mom for rescue.
She examined my suit, and me, declared, "It's here! Already!"
My period, an exclamation mark, a round of soda,
my feet propped, salty chips and a story before it was time.
My mother with a box of tampons in tow.
"It's easy, Ellen, you just pop it in."
"Pop what in?" "Where?" Locked in the bathroom,
the directions on the back of the toilet, my legs wide
I put the whole thing in, cardboard and all,
and declared, "I did it!" Then realized I didn't. So I
soaked in the tub, my body brand-new to me, my mother
on the edge telling how her sisters helped her and that since I
had none she was helping me. My confusion prompting
my mother to demonstrate the tricky tampon technique

using her own vagina. "Oh!" I hadn't realized. My vagina suddenly became a new thing I hadn't really seen at all. A new luxury of woman, a new thing to own, as my mother crowned me grown-up, crowned me daughter who could. And I could.

PUBERTY—WITH CAPITAL LETTERS

There went being a kid. There went
Barbie dolls, baby dolls, kitchen sets, play-
doh, crayons, make-believe (well, maybe not
make-believe). But there went innocent, child-
like, there went one-piece bathing suits. In came
adolescence, even though I'd had my period
since I was 10. In came self-consciousness,
waiting for breasts. In came attitude, and "Why
can't I?" "You said!" "I hate you," under my breath.
In came diaries with hidden messages and dares
I always took. In came kissing and not kissing,
and doing it, and not doing it, and rounding bases,
and not rounding bases, and rounding bases having
nothing at all to do with baseball, and sometimes wishing
you could just play baseball instead.

In came. Rebellion. Clichés. Are you kidding? Drinking.
Do-overs. Cheer-leading Uniforms. Regret. Pure Bliss.
Uncovering. Feeling not good enough. Cockiness. Joy.
In came wild cards. Short skirts. Cocktails. 15. Funnels.
Mid-riff baring. Belly-button rings. Challenges. Being
challenging. The ultimate change. The ultimate fast-forward.
In came growing up.

DRESS CODE

Cool, but not too cool. Chilled out. Yes. Cross colors, tight jeans. Can you master the tight roll? Can you rock a fat coat but still look skinny? Slim line style. Can you have 12 body-suits you bought from the mall? A blow-out, a ceaser, long braids, an afro, can you pick it out, wear it natural, frizz and groove. Slide. Can you act like you didn't take 90 minutes on your eyelids? Can you wax it, shave it, cut it off? Drag it behind you like fresh kill? Do you have style? Can you get it on, beat it til it hurts. Does it hurt when you look at yourself in the mirror? Ooooo, that hurts. Are you smooth? Can you dance? Electric slide boogaloo, the Janet Jackson Rhythm Nation—5, 4, 3, 2, 1. Can you look at all like Janet Jackson, or any one of her awesome back-up dancers? Did your uncles call you solid gold on the dance floor of a family wedding when you were five? Did you always think you were solid gold from then on? Can you running man, man, can you Roger Rabbit, Robot? Can you freestyle, shake your hair, look pensive like Mariah Carey, singing "Vision of Love" louder than your friends cause you've been listening to it longer.

Dress

Well. It's that, and more. It's can you roller skate? Do you have new wheels? Do they shine when they spin? Can you still eat a sno-cone and look cool in the 8th grade? Do you have anyone to slow skate with when "Lady in Red" comes on at Whispering Wheels? Do you skate by yourself because your best friend Britt, who has a bigger bra size and auburn hair like the deep rust of tress is slow-skating with the coolest boy? Do you skate into the bathroom and pretend to fix your hair? Is your hair un-fixable? Do you almost cry, but not really? Are you always hungry? Can you limbo? Do you say, "How low can you go?" and imagine you are funnier than you are. Do you play air hockey and act like you'd rather be doing that than skating with the cute boy? Do you imagine the taste of bourbon because you were born in its capital? Do you think it will make you prettier, smarter, act cooler, look more like a movie star, or Mariah Carey, or any one of Janet Jackson's back-up dancers? Will you have the moves when it really counts? Will it ever stop counting? 5, 4, 3, 2, 1.

PERSEPHONE MIXED UP

Loss of harvest, pomegranate seeds
never tasted 'til I was 23, winter comes
creaking, my bones grow cold.
Heartache around the corner, creeping
14, the Jersey shore and my vir-
ginity slipping out, into oblivion.
How I held my underwear and the
trees went bare, how the dark
howled and the snow fell. His name
tattooed on skin so dry. Wet ink
winter weeping. Tanned legs, what is
the harvest? A full belly, long kiss
that lasts miles, labor. Drives far
away, I've been under sea, under
neath, suffocated before.
Process of loss has been simple, has
been no phone calls, curled in bed.
There was no harvest, for men stripped
down me, the ripping wind, the cut
faces, the slashed tires, single bed, the
tequila and funnel, the stare down with
the mirror, analyzation of
skin, searching me, where is me?

THE BODY

finger
bone
breath
hair
hand
heart
hymen
veil
lingam
yoni
perpetually joined
mouth
lotus to open
vagina
mouth vulva symbolism
devours or possesses
bigger and rounder
fuller and louder
swallow whole
all of me in one gulp
yawning yoni
palm to sky
to chest
gates of hell
ready to swallow man
navel
center to bone and out

placenta

saliva

skeleton

skull, thigh, femur, length

of who I am

life force

caul

devour of men

fear inducing vagina

desired and tried to get to

to get at

plant of eternal life

womb

GIANINA BAZAZ. OR MOM

her nose is mine. the hook. slide.
the hump, then river of it. arab.

how many times do i claim it before
i am comfortable having it on my face?

her acne. back now. like hers, my skin
rages. chest. back. cheeks. neck. fore-
head. chin. nose. my god. my face,

a constellation. rugged with potholes.
the scarring marking me. my skin a design.
like hers. i see the deep pockets. the oil

slick we are. like me. like her.
my face. a map home.

OUR WOMEN

Wait until they come.
The gypsy women. Their
trunks on their backs, hard
shoes and sturdy legs, over the
miles. "You will be waiting for
them," my mother says at the kitchen
table, "yes, you will." They will travel
in packs of long hair, curled and weeping
down their backs. Oceans and rivers of hair.
They will have castanets that clack when they
come and wide as mouths dresses that will sweep
you underneath and never let you go. Playing palmas
and snapping their fingers slick and smooth, oh, they will
come crashing when they come. A whole universe of body
slapping and song. Their homes will be hillsides, the banks
of creeks, whole lakes. They will bring water and you will want
to be so careful not to drown. Humming will lift you. They will come
with their cheeks hollowed, but laughing. Their faces will look like
yours. They will come walking from Assyria, from the desert, and you
will be so thirsty and they will let you drink. They will come with noses
like you and jaw bones like you and faces too, but stronger. Fredida and
Razook will send them. And Albert Bazaz too. They will be covered in
the darkness of the land and they will want you to travel with them. "We
will sell you off to the gypsies," my mother says, "And don't worry, we
know them. We are them. So they'll come."

QUESTIONS

have me asking. how to keep my plants alive
make a good, strong cup of coffee, cook a chicken.

have me asking. how to skin a wolf. a cobra. the skin
from an owl. a pencil. the curve of confusion. if i had to.

how to roast a fish, pick its bones from my teeth. peel an
avocado. onion. un-ravel yarn. you. knit a sweater. do
the electric-slide. fix the water heater, make the bed,
do the dishes, do the laundry, tie a neck-tie, tie a rope,
patch a tire, cut the lawn, green and smelling fresh, ride
the train, play the accordion, hole the thread, mend the
break, bandage the wound, bind the sprain, cover the
damage. ask for it. make an excel spread sheet, match
clothes, keep warm. keep up. hold breath. have me asking.

how to raise a baby. the dead. a fist. the sky. how to win
monopoly. funnel a beer and not throw up after. how to
keep a job, lose one. start a fire. change the course of the sea.
be the sea. speak arabic. speak tagalog. speak spanish. speak in tongues.
let my tongue speak for itself. get un-tied. be tied up.

have me asking. how to chart the course. chart the answers.
chart my own destructive nature. hold on.

CONJWOMAN

drunk on the bourbon and the sugar cane drunk on the piñacolada
margarita hurricane sexonthebeach fuzzynavel blowjob bullshit we get
on every corner southern crawl full on shrimp and grits the okra in
the gumbo smooth lost bread oyster po boys from the acme pleasure
this act of want slippery insides the water is floating wanna swallow
it and chase it the levee breaks anyway beer stays cold from all the ice
chests bust open open call cloud of smoke up to my knees now to my
waist now can still swallow and wade now

new orleans i have been slow whispering your name i am thinking of
you and of us this steady slow grind we do we conjwomen dress all in
white carry prayers for marie laveau we women who study the spine
of want over red beans and pork chops strut wide open the streets
from decatur to rampart swing hips just right trombone trombone
slow slide of trombone all whipped with louisiana heat the cat sitting
stank in the box of peanut chews on the corner settin' spells lazy while
crawfish boil in a vat of salty garlic water slipping down below the
belly of want wanna come back here to you baby travel frenchmen
street to the praline connection where we eat fried chicken livers and
fried pickles and cajun fried catfish cold beer swallow all the hello's
swallow all the getting to know you's and slip into all the i want you's
we really wanna say anyway

want to take you home mardi gras beads and distance marking the
delta to the bluegrass the bayou to the kentucky river meridian to
maysville and back again and back again we swim rivers like the first
time pontchartrain biloxi ohio the wide of my back stroke ripping the

water onto the shore i can feel the beads wrapping themselves round
my neck can see your hands stretching can still open my eyes quick
out of breath and reaching

OLD BARDSTOWN

the wind whips hard electric, exhausted. it's old bardstown, it's country high-way, little boys with corn colored hair, it's mud-filled sundays and saturdays, it's the am and fm coming through, no tapes, no CDs. just open tar dividing trailer from beat-up truck, from doberman, from rusted up swing-set, from me. never did tell you i drove fast to get to you, peeled wide though every curve, my foot stayed gripped through whitney stables, american flags whipping viciously, crooked mailboxes, white crosses dotting front lawns, jesus statues. never did tell you i said hail mary 21 times, your name tripping space between, past the virgin who was warning me. never did tell you i could've loved you, might've, wanted to, real bad. oh, i wanted to, spread all five fingers out on the table next to your luke warm and weak tea. tell you my love woulda been bigger than any river you'd ever catch crawdads in. wanted to spell it out thick and wide across from your smile, from the artichoke dip we ordered, the food neither one of us ate, country ham, wheat bread, garden tomatoes, mayonnaise spread heavy. i only ordered to act like there was space next to my heart for food.

THE DISTANCE

there is blood on my tongue. releasing
your hand. if i could fit up to your wrist
in my mouth i would. walk into your out-
stretched fingers, let them be my buoy. i am
propelled by you. you are my ocean. i will
wade as long as it takes. scale walls. swallow
fire. you. there is blood on my tongue the color
your mouth. i open windows, the moon's got
your face in its grip. there is blood on my tongue.
i watch you leave, bullet prints on the side
your face, bullet prints marking you savage, you
un-revolutionized, you dirty, you hollow, you un-
masked, you beat. you a cloudy overcast afternoon.
you beaten with branches outside your home in the
country. on city streets. you no good. you hunted.
the law. your wrists. the jingle of sirens, your perfect
ears. i will place both palms over your face, keep the
soot from your eyes, shield them, the strength of my hands
there is blood on my tongue. i've tasted the metal door, your
heartbeat, the insides of your forearms. they're burning.
i'll bury them for you. i will walk across fire, and then back again
and then back again. i will wade in water up to my neck, keep it close,
i will wade, keep you at bay. i will call you past midnight, holler your
name up the creek-bed. holler
you home.

AUGUST

my mother and i shop for penne pasta and spinach / crowd
the aisles slow buy hummus and red wine vinegar / black olives
and red pepper / she tells me i am a broken woman / too dense
and dumb to notice / puts her skinny fingers round my neck near
the banana and mango stand / says this is what he will do to you
if you don't get out
her voice burns nectarine / fleshy / round /
full / bottomed
we drive slow / deliberate
home
past the chevron / and movie time
past home and garden / super wal-mart
two year olds swap secrets
and spit outside our front porch
we peel through the house together / her bony thighs knock
open the front door / hinges loose / she throws dwight yoakam
on the tape player / kicks her flip-flops aside / hums lightning
yellow through her lips / tells me to set the table / punchy
wine / salt / fork / knife / napkin / bolt / chain / my mother
uses her sharpest knife to slice tomatoes from her garden / i walk
by / test her kitchen sink / she places the sharpest knife in her kitchen at
my throat / says / this is what he will do to you if you don't get out
her voice drips tomato paste / thick
she slides aside / says sit
sit / enjoy / mangia / eat / eat / eat
men should never make you lose
your appetite

eat / eat / eat

fat portabella mushrooms dangle

chunky and smooth round her lips

she sucks in / tells me

do the same

my face squirms

our bodies fall

loose and heavy

wine is drunk

sauce is swallowed

my mother beckons me / calls me woman child still / warms her hands on my shoulder blades / wings / pats her thighs and pulls the strings of my hair / i sit / legs folded underneath / rag doll style / weak / my mother combs the tangles / french braids my hair / rocks me back / says she is sorry for me / that i am too naïve to be her flesh / not enough woman to be her womb / my mother puts her fingers round my elbows / brings my forehead / kisses it hard / rubs palms / kneads / tells me this is what he will do to you if you don't get out / and she lifts me off her hollowed lap / and she leaves / she leaves

I

I dreamt his arms hanging over
me like canopies, dreamt his fingers
loose linking spider webs, dreamt his
heart a fat pumping mouth chewing thick
strawberry bubble-gum, dreamt his smell of
dirt and wholeness, dreamt the jungle gym.
I dreamt myself into a moment, another time,
another picnic, in someone else's backyard.
I dreamt him and then me and then I did
everything to make him disappear.

YOU MADE ME THINK OF MY OLD LOVER

you made the muscles of his back blister in the shallow of my palm, made me think of his fingerprints, the smell of coconut oil that used to hold the thick plaits of his hair / you put that smell back into my mouth and it's getting to be like I can't even breathe anymore / huh-huh / huh-huh / huh-huh

maybe I wake up and he's standing over me, fingers inside my mouth, shoulder to shoulder eyes clear and smiling / and he's got his mouth on my appetite and I'm breathing in that stuff / his stuff / huh-huh / huh-huh / huh-huh / soft whisper and I am remembering his touch / and maybe he cries / or one tear wells up round the ring of his eye and I cry / or we just sit and he lets me fall in love with him / and he doesn't go away / and he doesn't force me to go away / and his smell stays on my skin even after I am rubbed raw

I still know it deep inside me / I remember country roads like this one / remember the dips / the crunch of sound as night moved into late / late night / country roads remind me of his tongue / long and perfect and on me / and my new lover tells me he doesn't think I need sex to survive / need sex to survive / need sex to survive /

and I want to tell him I feel like my body might rip open / that my stomach might bust up if no-one touches me / tell him I put my hands on myself so much that if I died the DA would know I killed myself cuz there'd be no other fingerprints anywhere near my body

I miss his mouth like I miss the cracking sounds of tree limbs near the river / I miss the insides of his skinny wrists like I miss the sound of 11 PM on a Saturday night in the deep / deep south / face out the window / stoned / I miss his fingers like I miss the length of I-75 / I miss him like home

that's how he comes to me at night / that's why when I dream of him I wake up wet and choking / why he's got his hands wrapped so tight round my throat that even if I wanted to call out his name / or YES / or NO / he wouldn't let me / I wouldn't try / and it's why I still can't write about him / why he is so crammed in round me that I can't move to get away / I want to see him the way I get thrilled by a full moon / the way I long to fall in love again / for real this time / that's how I know he's deep inside me still / embedded in me still

I want to uproot him now / want my underwear back / my writings / my fingerprints / I want them for me now / so please / please / don't tell me who I am or who you think I am or how much sex you think I need in my life / you don't know the hands that made fingerprints on me / you've never seen those fingers / never aimed at marking you whole

BREAK ME

I really need to know why we fall in love with men we know will break us, bones loose and shaking in our skin, rattling. Men who will make our bodies torn and bruised, blue, black, purple. If you hit me enough, I will be every color you want me to be. If you tell me you love me every time after your fingers have bruised holes in my mouth then I will start to believe you. I'll believe the marks; believe that you love me. You must. It's too warm to shut the windows. The ocean is loud like a stereo tonight and I can hear it all the way across the bay. You never call and I think you must be in the arms of someone who is not loving you enough. You're in the arms of love, the belly of want, soaking up his love. I want to tell you that I hope he is making you open your mouth, come loud as a fist breaking ribs, scream loud as a porch swing breaking off its hinges, legs spread and wide. gulley. bay. ocean. current. low-tide. gulley. Seaweed wrapped around your hands, handcuffed. I hope your body is popping louder than your mouth will be shouting to *get the hell out of my house.*

You are not a goddamned piece of shit, not a whore because you like it, not a slut, bitch, dumb ass pig. When a man calls you that you are not what he keeps saying. Send him back. Heal bloody, broken bones. Set them straight again. Hold them in place.

YOUNG THANGS

window reads stop the violence this is a drug free zone next street over
we see a forty in the backseat of a car the back windshield caved in on
itself from the pressure its glass warped and glossy this drugged up
violence all over covering we see a blue and white bandanna or some
young thang's dress dress up I wonder where is she now how high
her locks are swinging in what direction and how fast did the weather
wash her pretty sky colored dress or his slick bandanna how quick did
the water whip them up when 17th street became a river

the radio ripped out wonder what was playing maybe they were in a
slow creole moon groove dr. john's imitation of love his head thrown
back in a gut break type laugh or maybe this one rosie ledet song that
goes, "I want you so bad, I want you so bad and baby that ain't good"
maybe they were shaking loose to that and she was shooting him some
sick slick look, or maybe it was just the sound of a trumpet, slicing
through the august heat or maybe there was silence about to kiss
about to touch about to run or swim backstroke or butterfly

two lovers rushed clear out by water overflowing this sea the 17th street
levee made no elevation drunk on want and under water I'd have
liked to have been drunk too if I'd have known the water was rising
from creek-bed to sea if I'd have known the floods were about to sink
me and my baby my baby and the truth the truth and my one good
pair of red shoes hell my only pair of red shoes then there would have
been trouble but I'd have been knee-walking rowdy drunk cane sugar
lemon drop hallelujah drunk and I'd have been right there with my
baby too

II

I know the intimate lay of the sheets after they have been torn into, after the empty wet of the mouth has left stains, after the sheets are crumbled like a tangle of legs, after his smell stays, cookie-crumbs, a dirty sock, his blue sweater. After the presence of his has altered the shape of my room so that his mess is scattered around me like fingers locking into someone's hair. I kick him out and feel good. He is too preppy for me anyway. He's into stocks. He's into hair gel. He's into himself. So I open the door, his ass, the soft ball of my foot. *I'll never call* I want to shout. *I'll block all your calls. When I have enough quarters, I'll wash your smell out from my sheets.* On my way for bagels this morning I saw a dead pigeon. It made me think of my desire for you. You are not welcome here anymore.

PRAYER #1

the empty is the same deserted fleeing feeling of desperate is the same
lost vanity same soot scattered over no animals no children the same
no traffic no noise the same the same

and so i knew that smell neither of us turned away walked right up
to it a place with a queen sized bed on one side television busted up
on the other sure it was a man who lived there felt good and used up
smell neither of us turned away from I wanted to smell it even more
get the taste underneath and close to me so there'd be no chance to
forget this time

after september 11 when I lived in an apartment four blocks away full
of that same soot that same hot fine disaster I would wake in the
middle of violent sleep 3 am 4 am to that smell smell that you keep
tucked away forgotten until you're outside of some man's place in the
lower 9th with seering stomach cramps and it's 103 degrees under sea
level and that's where you're at you remember

there are clothes and papers scattered his personal things splayed out I
want to put them away save him from us watching who invited us in
here

in new york after it happened I wanted a warm bed clean underwear
and a bathroom after it happened I wanted to sit in it for hours
the next morning I stood in the underwear section of K Mart for
hours I settled on a pack of colorful Hanes Her Ways but greatly
underestimated the size of my behind they were so tight I had to trim

37

the elastic home in jersey my grandma offers her bra selection to me
she is a double D we eat greasy Chinese food

in new orleans we eat chicken livers and oily sausage gumbo the same
back on carondelet street we lay out on the bedspreads our clothes
damp and sticky we don't so much talk as we ly real still catching up
with breath that's been gone since we crossed over

III

It rained 'til I almost couldn't stand it anymore, rained so hard and for so long that it made my throat ache. I couldn't swallow; my throat felt swollen and it was always cold. That night I made popcorn. I watched one movie, showered and put on a pair of my mother's old cotton underwear. Every girl that I know; every girl worth her weight as a daughter has borrowed a pair from her mother. Stashed in her drawer, they're the last pair she'll wear, the haven't done laundry pair, the I'm not making love to anyone soon pair. They are the most comfortable pair; the ones that make you feel earthy, grounded. My mother's underwear is soft, smooth against my skin. I am closer to her when I wear them, the womb, closer to her physical body and I love that. That night I put them on happily, slid one leg in and then the other. I didn't go out. It rained so hard and I didn't feel like getting wet.

CRASH OF SLEEP

it is 7:30 am on the 4 train to the bronx we are heading fast uptown doors
swinging rough out from their sockets rush of burnside fordham road
kingsbridge terrace old armory dirt and trash mark the concrete below
me rip of train i sit next to a woman with the number nine on her chest
sprawling her breasts stretched her baby sleeps below sound no babies
lost intact still sweet asleep lavender baby bottles and satin blankets no
rush of nowhere nothing lost on this 4 train no stolen intake of breath
no thick water up to our waists just steady we both read the papers quiet
this morning does not erupt like we think it must baby names not old
enough to grow up we think unravel of wet dust the ocean is not near
enough for me to swallow it salt water sand castles bust wide open there
is not enough no wading no ankle deep no babies to find feet to grab
quick to we are just riding the 4 train mosholu parkway and dreaming
loose limbs to hang onto dreaming news we can read without our throats
burning and our mouths open screaming and wide without the heavy
soot covering us and the baby the baby sleeps we keep her that way

IV

I am different than I was five months ago. This is not the same desire at all, not even the same monster. It doesn't look the same, its eyes are different, its breath. At this point five months ago, I'd have written him a long love letter that smelled of me, something that made me cry while writing it. I'd have sealed it and then counted the days back from the one where I allowed myself room to want more. I'd have marked them off on the post of my bed. But that is not who I am, anymore. Tonight, I feel brave, feel like freshly poured cement smelling of footprints and dust. I feel like a newly washed, black shining car that's driving up midnight, the windows rolled down, air like a soft palm up against my cheek like a cradle. I am not a recovering addict. Let me be the first to say that I am still addicted. Let me be as clear as possible. I cannot be needing a man like you. At least that's what I say today, right now. Here, in this gravel. How quickly we forget one another's faces, how quickly we un-remember time spent with one another. I read your poems at night, poems that have most likely been sent up and down the mountain, have been in hands much more beautiful than mine, have kept women with much tighter bodies awake at night. But I do not long to send you my work. There is that piece in me that reminds me that I am not yours, that you do not own me, will never own me anymore.

TIMES

It is mid-morning
January, the heat
makes my shoulders pop
I drink coffee read
the paper disgusted
a leak of cinnamon toast
burgundy across the times
every-every-every
day we make excuses
rip up deadlines like
gulls of fish, caught
squirming, we exercise
our right to build walls
like loose spines re-connecting
in the body after being
crushed near beyond
repair. I take my luke warm cup
run it through the sink.
This is not sadness
that makes my mouth remember
dirt and metal
like my jungle gym,
I am wracked with fear.
My feet mark soft
along my wooden floor,
check myself out.
Today in the mirror,

a dull pair of child-sized
scissors in my fingers,
I cut my hair
for the decisions they are
making without me.
It's uneven I say,
twirl one whole,
fat lock round my index finger,
bring it to my nose.
It smells like woods
outside my house, Kentucky,
of charcoal, burning wood and VO5.
Hold it away from my face
examine its figure
in the mirror.
I lift my finger away,
but still holding on, I
run the dull blades through.
The hair responds quick,
prepared and falls
limp on the linoleum.
I pull another chunky lock,
twist and saw through, still uneven.
So I keep on.
My hair rummages around
in the sink like children,
confused and abandoned.
I can't get it even.
I can't remember why.
I keep on, chopping

maneuver through
like wading through salt water.
Strands falling 'til the belly of
my sink is stained deep brown.
I keep cutting,
apologize to my face.

V

What I know. I think I realized that nothing he ever said was going to make me feel any better. That it didn't matter what, that nothing I ever did, none of it would matter, that I would just be standing on the sidelines waiting for him. That maybe I had or have been doing that with so many men for so long. I realized then that it might not matter. That there were other things in life that I had, that there were other things that were better than any message he would ever send me or any time he would ever give to me. It would never be enough. He would never make me feel whole. And then, I realized that if I relied on every other man to make me feel whole I'd end up losing myself. I'd end up hating myself. Which I do not. This love is old, an old bag that's been sitting at my door. I haven't cried in 21 days, maybe longer really, but I know I have not cried in 21, have not spent days in bed with him at my door banging. My spider plant needs sunlight so I throw the windows open. I celebrate birthdays with good friends over good wine. I eat a steaming bowl of yankee bean soup at the heights diner every week. I teach 2nd graders to write about santo domingo that smells like summer. They write that their mothers smell like coconut and that this year they hope they will learn to count money. Every morning I drink a cup of earl grey with milk and sometimes sugar in the raw. I write. My sheets are almost always clean. Two nights ago I smoked weed and ate 'til my insides felt like a bear's in the middle of winter. It's the middle of winter. My roommates and I eat Ben and Jerry's half-baked right out of the carton. We eat Indian once a week. We go to the movies. I attend parties that are usually fun. I wear a hat all winter long. He will never be any good for me. Ever. I know. I just wanted to let you know that I know, too.

PLAN A

plan a he sees you in the hall. bright colors like tight fuschia. lime kicks. snug jean purple. so he sees you, smooth hair line, smooth skin, just past 14, on the f train, knee bending good looks, you've got him on like hooks, he slows down to a near crawl when he sees you in the hall, silk thighs, the white of your smile, smile wider, hips round up to waist, you move yours one inch closer every time you hear your name said right. he sees you in the hallway, gossip with your girls, grape bubble gum poppin', fingers, if you were lemonade you would be that cool, popsicles drip, you play yr cd player, 3 hole pierced ear jumpin'. so he calls you, "yo, what's up, can I get yr, digits?" yeah, so he calls you 20 times in like 15 minutes and you're like *yeah, whatever, yeah, whatever,* like you got day old rubber stuck to your gums. can he meet you in the evening when the moon is all dark, near the park, so y'all can mark body moves, trip space and time. your jeans rush you tight, cuz you like, no, love him. Feelin' up, feelin' down, break concrete, can't fall asleep, smack down, smack to in the middle of the country, plan a I tell you my dreams we watch movies, play ball, be-bop down the hall, your hand on my hip, you watch it shake, watch it shake, shake. short skirt, be all a flirt, like makin' mean egos trip. plan a you take me home. plan a I don't cry when I see you afterwards in the hall. plan a I call your house, leave long messages on your phone. you are always my home. me, never stranded, plan a.

RAPUNZEL REDUX

The girl
and she imagines how she will
save them all. her locks like
a buoy. who she will save
blow air in their mouths, if
only she wasn't locked in
some attic. waiting. waiting.
always waiting. there is no
he that can remove her from
her destiny. who would lock
her away anyway?

The hair
i am waiting for your un-leashing
thick, tied in a bun, heavy on
your head. i could save you,
i could cover the castle like
moss. you could braid
or plait me and i could be rope,
could be pulley, thick string,
i could lift them from the
water. could save
the drowning
the swallowing of sea.
if you just let me go, the
un-wind, i could be a
whip, the locks of a

chain. could hold onto.
could be pulled or pull
up from the deep end.

The boy
he will ask what is beauty
and see her locks traveling
down. her back, her waist,
the outward curve of hip.
intoxication, the orchids hanging
fresh in those curls, he will
want to wind himself inside
lose himself in those waves,
hang on and be saved. he will
want to know what does
it mean to be saved by a
woman's hair. thick river.
how it holds him firm.
how he is birthed again
in her warmth. he
will find himself in
trouble of getting lost
of losing himself, who
was he before, is he now.
caught on the railroad
of her. caught in her
magic, the conjure of
those flowing, that free
the unleashing of
that hair. he will
not mind drowning.

COUNT DOWN

Amaterasu. Aphrodite. Astarte. Artemis. Athena. Baba Yaga. Bast. Baubo. Epona.

Fortuna. Freja. Gaia. Ge. Hathor. Hecate. Hestia. Hina. Iambe. Inanna. Ishtar. Isis.

IxChel. Juno. Kali. Kwan Yin. Lilith. Maia. Medusa. Nuit. Oshun. Oya. Pallas. Pele. Persephone. Rhiannon. Spider Woman. Tara. Tyche. Venus. Vesta. Yemayá.

Amaterasu. Amanda Bynes. Aphrodite. Astarte. Artemis. Aniston. Athena. Baba Yaga. Bast. Baubo. Britney Spears. Condoleeza. Epona. Esotra. Ellen Degeneres. Fortuna. Freja. Gaia. Giselle. Ge. Goldie Hawn. Hathor. Hecate. Hestia. Hillary Duff. Hina. Iambe. Inanna. Ishtar. Isis. IxChel. Juno. Jessica Simpson. Kali. Kelly Ripa. Kwan Yin. Kelis. Lilith. Laura Bush. Lindsay Lohan. Maia. Madonna. Medusa. Mary Tyler Moore. Nuit. Oshun. Oprah. Oya. Olsens. Pallas. Pele. Paris Hilton. Persephone. Rhiannon. Spider Woman. Serena Williams. Tara. Tyche. Venus. Vesta. Yemayá.

Amaterasu. Amanda Bynes. Aphrodite. Anorexia. Astarte. Artemis. Aniston. Athena. Baba Yaga. Bratz. Bitch. Bast. Barbie. Blush. Baubo. Breasts. Bubble-Yum. Britney Spears. Condoleeza. Cunt. Curls. Coochie. Dyke. Diva. Desperate Housewives. Douche. Epona. Esotra. Ellen Degeneres. Fortuna. Freja. Gaia. Giselle. Ge. Goldie Hawn. Hathor. Hot Hair. Hecate. Hestia. Hilary Duff. Hina. Iambe. Inanna. Ishtar. Isis. IxChel. Juno. Jessica Simpson. Kali. Kelly Ripa. Kwan Yin. Kelis. Lace.

Lilith. Lesbian. Laura Bush. Lindsay Lohan. Maia. Madonna. Medusa. Mascara. Mary Tyler Moore. Nuit. Oshun. Oprah. Oya. Olsens. Pallas. Push-up bras. Pele. Panties. Pink. Paris Hilton. Persephone. Perfume. Queen of Earth. Queen of Water. Rhiannon. Spider Woman. Stilettos. Serena Williams. Skinny. Straight. Tara. Tyche. Tits. Venus. Victoria's Secret. Vesta. Voluptuous. Yemayá.

DEAR PRIVATE
FOR LYNDDIE ENGLAND

Girl, when I fell in love, I wanted to lay down tracks in skin too, uncover all and expose, wanted to say yes even when it was too dark, the ceiling too close.

Did the sky open crystal?
Did he fix you a large vodka and grape kool-aid to sip on afterwards?

Girl, when I was 17, I went to his house cause he told me to, but she was there and brought a knife out from the drawer to slice my face or my tires, either one, I left because he didn't get up from the couch, all legs long as summer days, watermelon Popsicles, front porches. I left because he didn't get up, but what if he had? Would I have stayed, her with blade, me with face? Would I have gotten cut for him, fought back for him, stayed under his roof, caving, in his room, forever, for him?

It's a long way from home, five months pregnant, leashes still in both hands, in dreams. Do you ever find your whole neck leashed? Are there ever bruises on backs of necks, earlobes, from all the fierce kissing, all the heavy necking? Hair cut short, you looked like a girl. Girl, do you still feel like one?

I am imaging the jump from my roof, all the wires we dodged two nights ago. I am imagining concrete, your breath, the way your breasts filled that shirt in your picture, the smile you had that made your left eye near close, wet drink in your hand, desert, bars, prison, leashes, fingers gripping him and a soda, kool-aid and cigarettes, back home, baby kicks, tv wails, every picture you see. I imagine it must be worse to just go home, wailing baby, tv kickin', too young to do shit. I imagine you get beat by someone, someone must make it too bad to go home. But didn't you imagine they'd find you? What made you stay so long? Short cropped hair, leashed thighs, vodka, new baby, tight jeans, general, white teeth. You look so happy. If I'd have stayed lodged under his roof, would I be pregnant and happy too? Dirty photos. Would I learn new positions, carry leashes, wear tight shirts, grow bigger breasts?

TODAY

because ache is real. specific. please. my jaw aches. no sleep. what is reckless enters in, and is. 6:30 am makes my eyes churn. 7:07 out the door. no food. a buttered roll and too strong tea from the cart on astor. the n train at 8th to 42nd. switch it up. take the 2 all the way to the deepest end of the bronx. almost wakefield. almost awake still. intervale, simpson. or simpson intervale. gun hill road. the stained glass everywhere. 219th. my i-pod trained to t.i. and rhianna and i feel teenaged, but my body, slow. lungs tight. near 30 in 12 days. dios de los muertes. these days i am teacher, am administratable, am wed. 217th at the forward school where the metal detectors beep. beep. beep. her shiny silver hip chain. his gold necklace. diamond earrings. his orange spider rings. her vicks vapo-rub. her tampons. her maxi-pads. his full bag of notebooks. her dignity. mine. shame. beep. like jail. beep. awake still. beep. 8th grade. there is a boy in the back named casey. long pony tail, and when the teacher says, "how you gonna pass english if you can't write?" he says, "i'm not english ms. i'm puerto rican," his smile like the fat half of a pie. he answers every question. blocks out the noise. the beeping. the principal coming in to say, "take your hat off. take your hoods off. take your jackets off." no hello. and i am only brief in my stay. talk to the artists. talk to the counselors. talk to the kids. julian shows me why she writes and her smile is a propeller. back on the train. i eat two veggie patties from golden krust because the feeding tree is shut-down and my favorite mexican spot was closed for health and mental hygiene. sometimes i think i might need to be boarded up, taken away for those very same. very specific reasons too.

TO MARILYN & LINDSAY

bless the milk and the raw
eggs. in the photograph, you
are blond curls, bouncing, bouncing
breasts, a high giggle, an itty
bitty waistline, dye job, lips
pouting, pomegranate colored
nipples, flouncing, free
"look at me."

in old photographs, you are holding
so tight, 36, and how do you
keep firm? how do you tease
men and the camera, the lens
and the world, your teeth
clinging, clutching chiffon, diamonds
in your cleavage, a come to,
a hither, oh how you play the
pin-up, how you push pussy, play
up promiscuity, primp,
pimp yourself for the fan, fan
dance, flirt, oh how you flirt.
for what?

and bless the new child, who
conjures your ghost, who wears
a wig and sucks in until her
waist is itty bitty too, who

bares breast and white teeth,
diamonds and chiffon, who
breaks down nothing, but
pushes that same, "come and
get it." if I take it off
you will look at me. please look at
me as I strip for you, my whiteness
like an antebellum phantom child
come a haunting. white
sheets to slink into, my
white behind, in white light
waiting for some white knight
to come and save me. "look
at me." pouting lips
and sunshine. it was the black
boys who done it. snorted the
coke, drove the car. oblivion.
lock them up in chains, behind
bars, take them away. "look at
me." the dye in my
hair runs free. my hair is
no longer auburn, it's
blond. my blond is no longer blond
it's platinum. my soundtracks,
my elaborate lies, my house in
the hills, my silk thighs,
and then you can't hear my
cries cause i'm all mixed up
telling little girls how to pose,
how to pin-up

how to strut. strut into
the light. keep on. keep on

bless you little girl. 21 and all
these tall tales you been told by
television shows, victoria's secret
by e true hollywood tales
by history, all this about
what will make the media
want me. it's a lie little
girl, because soon enough
you will be 36 and 56, and 76 and
then what will you do with
all that beauty then? when the
camera has fallen in love
with younger, firmer, bigger,
perkier? when men and women
fail to worship your hips, cause
your hips are old. how will
your mind, your brain, the muscle
of your heart take it when
they realize you've given them up
for plain and simple beauty?

DEAR CHRIS BROWN,

Has anyone told you, you should keep your pearly
teeth. In check. Your tattooed, muscled up
arms, covered. Your grin & dimple & hustle &
jet ski & Miami & showdown & Puffy & P. Diddy &
mansion on the beach & on the beach. Keep all
that under wrap. Come on. Write a letter to your fans
detailing the disaster. Look sorry. Be sorry. Look
devastated. Be devastated. Don't be sunscreen & jumping
waves. Don't be South Beach, pomegranate martinis. Cock-
tails & massages. Don't be wave jumping. Smiling. Your laugh
like a house on fire. Be real tears & locked in your bedroom.
Be love letters that last. Don't be bite marks & court records,
the record of her voice shouting for you to drive, or sing, or
do your Michael Jackson impersonator type moves. Or be pop
star. Be iTunes. Be fans in the stands. Milk ads where you
click your heels like Dorothy. Be double-mint gum & 19
Be 19. Boy. Be back to class, please, & teenager. College
courses. Not pummel. Shove. Fist. The tear of your fingernails.
Her heart. Her bloodied. Eyes. The puff & pout of her mouth.
Don't be fancy suit to meet the judge, & ironed white shirt. Stiff.
Expensive ties. The smell of your fresh breath. I was wrong. Be more
than sorry. Be crippled from your actions. Don't get out of bed, the
house, jail. Don't post bail. Sit in it. Wallow, or moan loud as it sounded
when your hits went #1. Look the part motherfucker. Look, you just
made me call you a motherfucker, motherfucker. & I liked your music.
You & R. Kelly both.

& Bobby Brown too. I first slow-danced with Nathan Farmer to Slow Dance in the 8th grade, & my best friend & I learned to smoke cigarettes & talk about boys to, "If it ain't good enough, good enough baby... I'll work harder." & I learned about kissing & my own body to 12 play. Loved that. Hard. But now I feel traitor, & devil when I listen, & think of that essay Mad at Miles, that I been meaning to read, cause Chris Brown, I am mad at you. You should know. Should post this letter up where you can see it. Read it. Be the kind of man I want you to be.

Not Yours (anymore)

Ellen

PLAN B

Plan B the doctor hooks you up.

One prescription.

Two pills.

Three days too late.

Four hairs you pull from your pretty, pretty head.

Five phone calls you've made in two days.

Six times you've cried.

Seven holes in the wall now.

Eight times your fist has ached.

Nine times you've called him a

"sick fucking piece of shit dumb-ass motherfucker!"

to yourself.

Ten hours alone, in bed, covers pulled up to your chin.

Eleven times you've pushed your stomach out in your bedroom mirror,

one time your mom caught you and you said you'd eaten too much at

dinner.

Twelve times you've lied now, to yourself mostly.

Thirteen, your age.

Fourteen days till school starts.

Fifteen hours of watching MTV in one day.

Sixteen ways to kill yourself, and maybe two ways to kill him.

Seventeen magazine arrives today to tell you all the ways to protect

yourself.

You can't depend on one.

A FACEBOOK STATUS UPDATE POEM

Ellen just woke up.

Ellen's hair is a mess.

Ellen's brushing her teeth.

Ellen loves Crest.

Ellen has sleep in her eyes.

Ellen's eyes are sore from partying. Yeah!

Ellen is tired still.

Ellen loves her bed. Ahhh!

Ellen's eating Cheerios. Smiley face!

Ellen's not on a diet. Hell no!

Ellen likes to refer to herself in third person.

Ellen just got out of the shower.

Ellen uses Dove soap.

Ellen's already bored with the day.

Ellen loves the sunshine.

Ellen just boarded the train.

Ellen is not sure where she's going.

Ellen is thinking about getting lost today.

Ellen reads the paper, thinks swine flu is a joke.

Ellen loves pigs, and bacon too.

Ellen wants more time off, a day at the beach.

Ellen's thinking of getting a Twitter account.

Ellen wants to tweet.

Ellen'll say things like: Ellen likes the smell of fall,

do you?

Ellen'll find out what Ashton Kutcher and

Oprah and the ladies of the View do

with all their spare time. Ellen will
follow the lives of Paris Hilton and Demi Lovato,
even though Ellen's not totally sure who
Demi Lovato is, but Ellen's former student,
who corrected Ellen when she kept saying twitters,
knows, and so Ellen is thinking of becoming
uber-uber-uber-connected, technological
porn. A day at the computer and nowhere
else to go. No one but Ellen. All Ellen. All
the time. All vanity. Obsession of self.
Ellen's eating lunch.
Ellen's riding the train home.
Ellen didn't run away.
Ellen's working out on the elliptical trainer,
and texting her inner-most thoughts.
Ellen's reading 30 poems in 30 days.
Ellen's trying to play catch up.
Ellen's exhausted.
Ellen's all status-ed out, all
twittered out. Ellen's going to sleep
to dream of witty, smart updates to pull
people in. Get 'em hooked.
Ellen's wondering if anyone is listening, or
paying any attention at all.
Ellen is really kind of sick of herself.

Ellen misses voices. The simple sound of
hello. And yes. She misses that too.

PLAYGROUND DREAMS

girls in the yard. hop
scotch baby on a tuesday
afternoon. knee-high bobby socks
girls with high pony-tails and plaits,
neon orange. aqua. leopard print style
and the beat goes. and the hands
go. and the snap. and the run, run
run around. and their curls fly, their
fly, tight pants tumble up.
sky. style. estilo. the open road.
schoolyard. four roosters, and no
way in. out. bed-room, bed-rock,
all politics lead back. hop. scotch.
on a tuesday. throw the stones. tuck
the knees. keep jumping girl. higher.
higher.

ODE TO PS 315

With its no windowed walls
there's never been a time I've felt
caged in. Comfortable. Always.
As 7th graders snort snot back
into their heads, fix fashion,
be fashionable, or not, be fly, be
tight yellow jeans and tank tops.
No uniforms here. The dress code un-
coded, gone like the chill of January,
glad it's spring. Warm breeze
and cafe con leche at El Liberato
on 183rd. Been thinking
of 13, the age, the number, and how
it must be wicked. Young people
setting spells, becoming lean, be-
coming up in years. Older. Older.

Their sneakers: fresh. Their faces:
broken out. Like mine. Their language:
fire. No, that's cliché. Like them. Their
words: the hot sauce on the tongue, the
rising solitude of teenager.
Their new looks, new highlights, new smoothed
out hair-dos, their suits and
jackets, high-topped, silver hooped.

Crescendo. Pencil bags and
posters of the world. Their
purple and pink, their colors so pre-
pubescent. Their lunchroom riots
over green beans and chicken patties.
Whole milk and not getting the boy.
Boy. Girl. All these hormones like lost
fingers. Reaching. The open-i n g
up of hearts, spines. Loosened up
in the skin. Lungs of them spread.
More breathing space. More exhale.
All that is good. Oh, PS 315, how I
dream of ways to get you
to speak all these things.

PS EDUCATION

Take all the metal detectors apart and build imaginary cities with them. Then my 7th graders can build a utopia and walk around in it. Tell Harold, the security guard, who sings only Tito Puente songs, that he can have his own music room, and buy gold trumpets and trombones that slide like hot oil. Buy drums that rumble the whole school: da-dum, da-dum. Build a garden as big as the football field at Taft High School and feed everything. Tell Myles he can have a quiet room to fall asleep in, because I know he is tired. "I know you are tired, Myles, but you cannot keep calling Russell a fat fuck, "Yo Russell, you fat fuck," over and over until Russell has to stand up and punch Myles where he deserves it most. And why not? Call Russell a genius, who sure knows how to write about his grandma and the shiny wheelchair she rolls in. Tell Shelquan to get down from the air conditioner. He is singing, "This is why I'm hot," with sunglasses he stole from Crystal, whose best friend Kiara has carved the word HATE in her arm. Remind Crystal and her girl Kiara that a woman should never mark her body with a word meant to destroy. Yell at them loudly and when Crystal's nana shows up at the school, tell her anyway, even though she does not speak English and Crystal might not translate. She might. Tell Yaneira that she is a hot skillet when she writes, and not a "retard," which is what Eduardo calls her under his breath. A fire woman. Really. And when Fatumata stops you in the street in front of the McDonald's to say good morning, tell her she is late again, but yes, good morning. And tell her to get out of 339, or ask her to help you make it better. You know she can. Listen to Racheal's poem over and over again. She needs it when Angel, who you cannot believe has turned on you, makes fun of the lilt in her voice, stare him down with your witchy eyes. Tell him, teach him how to say, "I will look at you Racheal and I will see you," 1,000 times over. Racheal, where Trinidad and Guyana meet. Tell her the truth, that you never knew where she was from until you asked, and when you finally asked it was way later than you wanted. Put the principal in class with all the run-down teachers, no pencils, paperless notebooks. Don't give him books because you know he is lazy. Call him lazy. Because he is. Make him walk in and out of the metal detectors, saying, "Next school year I will do better, and serve you better." Make him mean it. Show up. Pencils and papers at the ready.

POSITIVE BEGINNINGS—CHILD DEVELOPMENT
CENTER—1130 LIZARDI STREET—944-CARE

i wonder who is gonna call now? now that there in no phone in the phone booth. been ripped out nine months now. and next door has got bullets on the front porch. littered with shine. who needs child care when the schools are wrapped with tree limbs, rubble, dust. Louis Armstrong Elementary has had no dial tone since August. no boxes of chocolate milk, no freeze tag or hopscotch and what about the books? where have they been washed off to? now, only classrooms upturned. there is no healing over yet. no pick up, cleaned out. no clorox or bleach here. only mold growing along the walls where the alphabet used to be, and the times table. who needs child care when the roads are empty of hot red roller skates, bicycles and shouts to, "come on out!" to where? for what?

Kenneth Reed sat at the first table. his name tag still intact. the glue and tape were his. his board games. his art hanging loose on the walls. wherever he is. Texas. Atlanta. Florida. Alabama. he wants them back. wants his chair covered in rust. he thinks of home not like this. but in color. the electric blue paint still out on the table. once fresh. soft yellow football with Zulu written on it. the deep brown of the African masks, one on each side of the doors. a blue stamp, the ink still wet. the mobile the babies would look up at as they fell asleep. he sees in color. images that break him away in slow, steady grips. even if he wanted to call home. he couldn't.

ROLE-CALL

Talia. Astrid. Azel in Far Rockaway. Mergim on 22nd and Lex. Mauricia. Menaka. Jasmin. Chasity. The girls. Girlstory. SOF. 132. 27. 339. BWA. Ting. Harlychak. PS 360. Down a long road. Kingsbridge Terrace. Rooster school. Red Hook. Fordham Road. Burnside. Mosholu Parkway. Tracey Towers. Defeat. Othello. Numb asleep. Rodell. Blue pen. Vomit. Washington Heights. Sadeghi. Bright hot pumas that pump when you step. Two-step outside on the concrete. Cell phones in earringed ears. Martin. Del Villar. Sosa. Stone. Ramos. Polland. Akeem. Antoine. Daysia. Deasia. Donasia. Nyasia. Lynasia. And Asia. Kingsly. Kiara. Christopher. Mohamado. Jester. Gennder. Julisa. Jeanice. Joleany. Jairo. Herminio. Hannah. Hip-Hop. The Bronx. Birthplace. Bling! Bling! Bling! Brooklyn-Queens Expressway. Twice on Thursdays. 17th street and 4th avenue. Park Slope. Carroll Gardens. Smith and 9th. 183rd St. Tacos Neza. Un taco de queso por favor. The only thing I could order in Spanish. Belmont Branch. Arthur Avenue. Italian grocery with bottle of coke-cola. Watermelon Icees at Sorrento's. Hernandez. High. Prince. Ocasio. Gil. ACTION. Dreamyard. CWP. Aracelis. Lola. Lisa. Nikki. Rachelle. Streets that lead me back again. Manhattan. 167th street. 149th and the ocean. The ocean between us. Beach street. Empty and abandoned. Kennedy's Fried Chicken. The BX12, the BX11, the BX9, the BX35, the BX42. Riverdale and West Farms. West Tremont. The Bronx Zoo school where they made coffee with steaming milk for me on Mondays in May and June. Claremont Parkway. TYWLS. Rebell. East Harlem. Shake-down. BET building. 106 & Park. Naquan. Daquan and Malquan. Mr. Charles. Ms. London. Ms. Sutherland. Mr. Joe stoned as the asphalt. And hello? And hello? PS 32. Senator. More coffee. Names of students I cannot remember. Who are they? Shaquarius. Shameka.

Shawn. Shakim. So tired my whole body lifts awake on the train. Struggle to hold onto their names. Caridad. Rice 'n Beans every week. Shovel. Mouth. Platanos. Madurros. The A to the F to the A train. The 6 to the 4 to the D train. The D to the 4 to the 6 train. The F to the D to the BX11 bus going all over town. Pit-bull giving birth on the sidewalk. I wonder sometimes how can I come back here? How can I not?

WHO HAS LOVED YOU? LOVED YOU UN-STOPPABLY?

My mother. Un-stoppably,
her face in my dreams, curve of her
smile. She has loved me after I've gone
and broke all her bones and the veins
to her heart, and her heart too. She
loved me when I lied, loved me when I was
reckless, tornado girl, child of hurricanes,
disaster of me. Loved me un-afraid even,
her face at the window waiting for her
daughter to return.

The empty break-dance of lungs, breathing
in, no air, just gasping of chest. The old heave,
pressure she must have felt, her longing like
some pastime she was perfecting. Her skills,
sensational. My mom, drowning in it.
She, she, she loves me.

HAGAN BORN

My father is a country boy. Slick hair. Shine of him. He's been drinking beer since he was 13. Fresh out the keg. He grew up fast, seven brothers and sisters. Corn on the cob for a whole meal. Church every morning. 7 am Jail twice for fist fights. He smokes cigarette after cigarette. So tipsy he loses his car on his first date with my mom. Holds his lighter up and tells her it's cool. He wears thin jeans, wavy hair. He's got a mustache and tight arms. He loves the way she talks. Loves her short hair-cut, her bright colors. She can dance. He wears white t-shirts that hug him. He asked her to slow dance even though he wasn't all that good, promised her a ride in the country. She was a girl from up north. A classy girl my father used to say. There are letters. Acres of letters. 800 miles of words between them. My mother says they fell in love easy. My father was a good-lookin' country boy from New Haven. Shine of him. Liquor and bourbon of him. A rowdy, drinkin' man, but a good one. Only one of his friends to make it out of New Haven. He promised my mother he'd be there always. My mother was used to good things. She got used to him too. Quick.

MEMORARE

My mother's hair is cut short, shorn. She says open-heart surgery prepares you for death. She's been packing the house. It was only little trinkets at first and she started in her bedroom. All the pictures of our family in one drawer, all the pictures of our friends in another, piles and piles of old photos that told stories she wasn't sure she'd ever tell again. She'd look at one, then look at me and hold it up to the light. This picture told a good story, she would say. I am sorry no-one will ever tell it to your children, if you ever have children that is. My mother believes in packing things away, believes in trunks and suitcases and deep wooden drawers. She believes in closing things up, tying them down, stringing rocks to them and dropping them in the riverbed. She's been packing up her clothes too, and her little soaps and her lipstick tubes and compacts. She put her Daily Prayer Book and her Heart of Jesus Pamphlet in a shoebox with her cross of Jesus Christ and sent it to me in New York fed ex. It arrived today. In a week the doctors will slice her chest open, cut between her rounded breasts, through her ribs, and stop her heart.

On the inside of her Saucony shoebox, was written the Memorare:

Remember O most gracious Virgin Mary that never was it known that anyone who fled to Thy protection, implored Thy help, and sought Thy intercession was left unaided, Inspired with this confidence, I fly unto Thee, O Virgin of virgins, My Mother! To Thee I come; before Thee I stand, sinful and sorrowful. Oh Mother of the Word incarnate! Despise not my petitions, but, in Thy mercy, hear and answer me. Amen.

DIS-MISSLE
FOR SARAH PALIN...AND HER PUNK ASS

and with the simple bat
of an adorned eyelid, lashes
aflutter, her whispers of yes.
of maverickness, maverocity,
mave-diocre. mayhem, and the
hem of her dress is let go,
let out. the chickens
in the coop. have flown.
are flying now. her hair
whipping like some wind
machine in yogurt ads, or
some commercial dedicated
to clean toilets, or un-
blemished kitchen counters.
count the number of times
her comb goes from scalp to tips,
frosted, like Alaska, there is no
fire for her, or warmth, no coal,
clean or otherwise, is coal
ever clean? do the bombs
ever explode on silent ears?
is there ever screaming that no-
one hears? hear this governor.
hear baghdad. hear tikrit. hear
the tigris river shake earth. and abu
dabi. hear the skyscrapers in dubai
place windows in buildings like

delicate bones. hear saudi
children. hear the marching of
machine guns. hear moustache
on east 10th street. ouzi's and
grilled lamb chops, hear my pop
open his grave to yell stop, and god-
damn. hear his skin break. hear turkey.
and syria. hear jordan. hear iran.
hear arabic. hear muslim. hear christian.
hear you tell it he a terrorist. as you
shine your weapon. gleaming. as you
sharpen your teeth. hear you tell it
he hussein. he muslim. he bombs.
he threat, as you fasten your holster,
and you dress in your clean pastel, and
you wink while holding the grenades that
drop from your french manicured fingers
into lands my people call home. call
home governor. remember that you
are not the only one who has one.

JACKSON, TENNESSEE

forget the phone call that did not wake you.
forget you were awake already. the officers on
the other line. forget their questions. dental records.
receipts. missing teeth. blisters already on hands.
forget how you heaved, your breath lost
feet un-steady, not your average anything
forget steadiness, that trip down south. forget
the ocean, the feel of his hands. his wedding band. all are
lost now. some highway has eaten them. greedy interstate.
forget that you wailed at the tar. told it where to put
all your pain. forget guacamole and steaks. there will be no
more bourbons or house calls. or calls on the phone. forget
the train that never stops, that never comes. the red lights
marking the distance. forget that the weatherman predicted snow
and it never, ever did. pull the curtains down. wallow thick and
deep if you have to. forget what is right. reason. logic.
all you realize, are not worth much.
anyhow. after. all.

QUESTIONS II

I am prepared to answer one question and one question only. It has nothing to do with Cuba. Or mojitos, and though I know more than I thought about it, no, I am not prepared to answer any questions about cerveza. Cristal, Bucanero or otherwise. The government. No officials. No preguntas on Che's love life, or after-life. No, none about the shape, taste of mint crushed with azúcar. None about sugar. Diabetes, or addiction. No pro-photo preguntas. Or ones about Santería. Or the size of Changó when he changes sky. Or the way Oya's hair whipped at Callejón de Hamel. None about where Yemayá lives in Havana Viejo. None, not one about Spanish, or Hemingway, or the Atlantic, and how many fish, bodies, rafts, motors, crabs, shrimps, octopus, or other five-legged things get caught, or don't, between the Florida Straits, and the coast of Havana. None about the Malecón, or gay life or the way french fries and black beans are Cuban American as well...I don't know. Again, none about the way a ceiling fan changes the light of day. Afternoon. Or Afro-Cuban Música. Or any music at all. No, I can't talk about leaving town, or borders. Or the way we connect, re-connect. Turn-off. Computers. The use of technology. The way sweat sticks to skin. Or drag queens in Pinar del Río. Swimming off the coast. Crumbled buildings, The way Cuba is Kentucky. Is New Orleans. Is Southern. And Island. And feels like. Home.

THE TACO POEM

FOR TACOS NEZA ON ST. NICHOLAS IN WASHINGTON HEIGHTS.

desire then, is two tacos.
one thick with fried cheese
the other chicken, salted, greased
perfection. warm home-made (and i
can see her make them) tortillas
bubble, rise in the oil. how every,
every week after teaching three ram-
bunctious, rowdy classes of second
graders, all i want is to be left alone
with my two tacos. the salsa picante
dripping from the palms of my hands,
the guacamole. the raw onions.
cilantro. cilantro. you beg me. my
mouth is yours. tongue. yes, that
too. i want nothing more than some
alone time spent with both of you,
so my pleasure can't be interrupted
by average, plain talk. no words please,
please don't mess my taste-buds up
with your simple language. i want
to close my eyes, weep if i want
when i bite into you. two tacos, you.
want no eyes on me, just me. maybe,
the juke-box tuned to a slow jam, or
some latin jazz. but i want to devour
messy like, swallow in ugly gulps,

get my fingers, hands, all drenched
in your taco bliss.

SWEET, SWEET
FOR DAVID

you are my mango. my slices of orange.
juicy. syrup sticking under fingers. palms.
my ruby-centered guava bursting taste-buds,
the sour skin of a plum, ripe, just letting in.
pulp. sour pull of pink grape-fruit. the work
of pomegranate, peeling away the skin. tangerine.
tart of strawberry. explode of taste. you are
my nectarine. your skin the fur of a peach just
plump, just dropping heavy from the tree. the
fleshy feel. cantaloupe. honeydew. you are
the heaviness of watermelon on a saturday after-
noon the crushed sugar of jam on my breath
after i've tasted all, all of you. crushed
under the weight of my tongue.

THE MAN

when we meet it is early
in the new year. a blizzard, up-
wards of 13 inches. snow for days.
he was consistent in his want
a telephone up-turned and him
on the other line, the dip
and slide. he was a con-
stant. a constellation. the sway
of an arm. slung.
the explosion, a
cheeseburger, flesh.
the juicy rawness. a flavor
i'd been too long without
and he never left.
followed me to
barbecue and the blues. memphis.
where i imagined him curled
and sleep in my arms.
how I'd never dreamed
him until he showed.

ADOLFO & JOHANNY

Adolfo had no fear.
He didn't care that we were all around him.
A jumble of maybes or noes all possible, still on his
mouth, a yes, teeth full of yes, a comfortable word, and
"I like your name. Johanny."
"Such interesting names," he says, his cap low.
She smiles. Hers is a mouth full of chocolate cupcake.
Her braces full of disaster. I move to tell her, "Johanny, there's
something in... then wait. She is full of no fear too. A team.
The D train bumps uptown,
traveling the light between 34th, 49th and Rockefeller Center,
125th, 135th, 145th he must be holding his breath, "I like
your earrings Johanny." Her name like a flower blooming
on his tongue. A whisper so sweet. I think the train is moving
so fast. He says their names, the girls, a chant...
"Johanny. Haydil. Miosoty.
Johanny. Haydil. Miosoty.
Johanny. Haydil. Miosoty."
His own, an answer. A prayer.
Adolfo, Adolfo, Adolfo, I am!
We all sit around the train rambling. Smile. He says,
"Goodnight," and I hope for a stall. The conductors voice.
A door jammed open. A bonfire to distraction. The clear end of
a tunnel closed off. Because I too want to be 13 again.
Braces and bad skin. A boy, about to profess, about to climb
the high dive. A crowd of on-lookers. A burst through. An
opening up of. A satisfaction unlike any. Newness as fresh

as the first time. A multitude. A quickening. A deepening. A thrust. A fist. A hello. A plunge. Adolfo. Johanny.

No lifeboat. No pair of swimmies.

Just Yes Yes Yes

THINGS TO TELL ARACELIE

When Aracelie is born, we will tell her
the story of her namesake, her great-grandmother,
died of pneumonia, so young, her deep black hair
tied up tight, child-like face. Married to Dominador
Alvarez Flores, who died at war. But no-one found
his body and so his ghost could be floating through the
islands, could not even be a ghost.

We will tell her of the warrior dance from the Philippines.
Stories I have not yet heard, but we will learn them,
and tell them. Her pop will tell her stories of how she became.
Her Filipino, Assyrian, Irish, Italian, German self. Her a mix
of lands and places she will travel. Names. Addresses she will un-fold.

We will tell her of Hebron, Indiana. Chicago blues,
the mid-west and Flornez her great-grandmother, dead
now and the way she sat tall and striking at the counter
in the old photo. World War II and how the soldiers
when they come back, they come back changed, ghosts of
themselves. They come back with bullet hole wounds,
lost limbs that ache when it rains. Ghost limbs.

We'll tell her of Paul and Miriam, whose name she too will carry.
Miriam Aracelie. Of the Kentucky hills, of the villages in the
Philippines, of the Irish green spring, of the dust marked Middle-
East, of the carrier of all things. Of salty fried cornbread and
grape leaves, of sweet empanadas and home-made ravioli at the

kitchen table in Dumont, New Jersey, of adobo and fresh garlic,
cilantro, oregano and Guinness. Beer and consumption.
Tell her of government jobs. Jobs spent hours and hours.
Jobs in the factories. Bourbon surveyor. Surveyor of all things.

Teach her to taste slowly. Consider her face, her hair,
the ghost limbs of her own. Teach her language and
how to weave stories like heavy, woolen things meant
to hold, meant to encompass, envelop, enclose. Take in.

FELISHA & MAR-E OR FELICIA & MARIE

either way, i've never heard their names
the lilting isha, or icia, or the mar, long e
until tonight.

three bourbons (just bourbon, maybe a lick
of water) for my father, two beers for me
we are what you would think of if you
were to think of pairs.

"i was the kind of guy who'd go
anywhere," my father tells it, re-
vealing three prom shots from 1967
and on. "i just wrote that in a poem,"
i state. keep on. like him.

"my great aunts, felisha and mar-e. nah
don't have a clue to the spelling, but
one was a post mistress and the other
run the dry goods store in new haven.
old maids the two of them. shared that
twin house in new haven. 'sides the church.
used to be i'd get a hershey's for free.
hell, we never had candy back then. i
mowed their yard. they kept a car.
neither could drive. had it in the case they
ever needed taken somewhere. i'd drive.
i'd go anywhere."

if there'd been a case of bud, i'da drunk
every last one. "what else," i say, "i've
never heard this many stories. where've they
been sleeping?"

my father says the kentucky, the new
haven, the irish, the country, the liquor, the
old town, the back woods in him has all
the time said to never let too many cards
un-fold. never show a full hand. not
never. so he is starting to forget that
he says. just now he is beginning the roots
of storyteller. i open wide both ears for the taking.

IN LOVE, WE DRIVE

He only ever wants to photograph
my hands. We are driving up from Memphis.
Barbecue, semis on the highway. He plays
James Brown on the juke-box. We travel roads
for the first time. I reach for the collar of his shirt,
something for me to grip. Hand him slices of clementines.
We roll down the windows. It's Tennessee hot
for this time of year. Snapshots.
Roll. Farms. The hills of this want run thick.

BACK AGAIN

been thinking of the land.
what kind of soil, red earth, clay
is out there. missing me even. of
where do we return to, and how long
it is we're s'posed to be gone. agrarian.
mountain-top. biscuits, the farm, and though
i've never been farmer, never been up at dawn

work the body, work the feed, work the horses, work the cows, work the
tractor, the hoe, the top and grow. work the body, work the body, work
the body. no, never worked. like that.

never stripped tobacco or planted a
thing. not one. even the two plants
on my east 7th street windowsill are
dying. a slow un-ending death under my un-
trained hands. not ever enough water, or
dirt, or a big enough pot to grow

just the same, i've been thinking on
figuring out how to make a thing sprout. ascend. propel from bottom.
how to make a thing widen into rows of another thing. sunflower. orange
blossom. corn. sugar cane. okra. hemp. the last like a rope always tying
me back.

been thinking of where i'd like my own ashes
scattered. which land, which river, body of water.

like yemayá. can i be of sea? and who am i like
if i am like red dirt. clay. which side of me. is that?
which side of me. is home.

EL FAROLITO

24th and Mission, a distance
not traveled yet. In love, we
order burritos, our voices low over
the aching music. An order of Coronas
so cold they burn. Me, vegetarian
him, chicken grilled slow. It drips
la tortilla, sour cream, soft black beans
and we're in love, Mission style
love, El Farolito on a Wednesday night,
a jukebox and a 12 year old girl in front. She
is eating vicious. An oxen. Or
boar. Her face a pink glisten.
Surrounded by cousins. Or Brothers,
or kids next door, she weighs
double what they do. All put in
together. She is a house. A mile. A
truck moving. I am astounded by
her. Keep turning around. She dips
la tortilla in green salsa so hot
I put my tongue on the beer bottle when I try.
She dives her mouth in, slurps the bottom
when she is done scraping and sopping with
la tortilla. Oh, what hunger you have got.
12 at El Farolito in the Mission. Her cousins
scoff, look at her, laugh. She takes them in
her jaw. Drags them loose. Her hunger
is electric. Is mean. Is uphill with no relief.

A machine, a roiling. I can see her appetite
from my seat, and silently put my hands together
and pray for 12 year old girls who know
what a full stomach feels like. Order another
burrito, stuffed at the waist. Silently mouth to her
"Keep on eating girl. You are a book-shelf, a
refrigerator bursting open. A full meal.
The price of falling.
Keep on, keep on, keep on eating,
girl."

IF NAMES WERE PRAYERS

FOR MY OLD/NEW STUDENTS FROM PS 315, BRONX, NY

shaheim hanley. daisy santos. carolina blaco. saleh fata. guadalupe
grande. erika mounier. esteffany martinez. jamel allen. eliani santos.
edgard bocio. dennis martinez. ali khan. angela cruz. and on. and on.
hands. palms facing in. the bowing, the crossing. the fingers spread, the
ashes. the chorus of song.

shaheim hanley. shaheim
is the wind for sure. sh, a whisper. ah,
the sound of a peeling fruit, mango, sha-
heim, the hem of a dress, the mellow
melt-down, lazing, lounging, an out-
back name, shaheim, a slow hustle, a
game of darts. sh, the sound of quiet,
crisp air. sha, song. some reggaeton,
shaheim, the long bus ride.
home.

guadalupe grande. big. big. big. beach
ball, the wide sun, a full, fat rainbow slurpie,
guadalupe, the sound of grapes growing
from earth. guadalupe like the rolling of
marbles, marmalade, maravilloso, the new
words i am rolling around. the tread of
sneakers. grande, the world, a mix of letters
that drop like avenue blocks under my feet.

ali khan. ali. a-li. ali khan. the distance, a
wide measuring device. ali, the zoom of the
number 4 train, frequent flier miles, wings, of
planes, of birds. ali, the settling dust if it
settles at all. khan, coffee beans, khan, thyme,
smashed garlic. ali khan, elementary, the
simple lay out, the un-complexity of language.

and there are more. names walking stride through my busy, busy mind.
continue. and on, and on.

THAT GIRL

i am no longer that girl. that girl
was a buck, she rode devils, she
wore short skirts that showed some thigh,
too much, she played ditch, double trouble,
skipped double dutch. she did him wrong
and her best friend wrong and her mama
wrong. she wore tight shirts that showed off small
breasts, she was country. she was treeless branches,
drank gin and miller high life, and she shook
her hips like this and she shook her hips
like that. she was the black bird
and the sun. she spoke woman tongue, crawled
'til she had grass stains melt on her belly. she took
her first curve fast, she was a fast talker, she wore bells,
drank her thick coffee brown. she played the afternoon
like it was her boyfriend coming home. she called him
sweet sunshine, rain, called him up one way and down another.
boyfriend! called him baby cakes, honey bun, angel,
she called, her high voice high, loud. she was the afternoon,
the town store that sold pecans and sugar sticks,
wore her uncle's cowboy hat, spit tobacco. she was
the picnic and the quilt spread lazily on the bed. she was
the stone he threw in the creekbed. she was bed post and
her mama's best helper. she was turtle road, holy cross church,
and the cash variety store. she was every road that led her.
she was home.

ELLEN HAGAN is a writer, performer, and educator. Her poetry and essays have appeared in literary journals, magazines, and anthologies. Ellen's performance work has been showcased at the New York International Fringe and Los Angeles Women's Theatre Festival, among others. She has received grants from the Kentucky Governor's School for the Arts and the Kentucky Foundation for Women, and she has held residencies at Hopscotch House and Louisiana ArtWorks. Ellen holds a BFA in Theater from the University of Kentucky and an MFA in Fiction from The New School in New York. A proud Kentucky writer, she is a member of the Affrilachian Poets and Conjwomen, and she is a co-founder of the girlstory collective. *Crowned* is her debut collection of poems.

www.ellenhagan.com

CPSIA information can be obtained at www.ICGtesting.com
Printed in the USA
BVOW070056120712

294965BV00001B/13/P